death is a mariachi

death is a mariachi

Poems

marcy rae henry

Bauhan Publishing
PETERBOROUGH NEW HAMPSHIRE
2025

ISBN: 978-087233-398-7
Library of Congress Cataloging-in-Publication Data

Names: Henry, Marcy Rae author
Title: Death is a mariachi : poems / Marcy Rae Henry.
Description: Peterborough, New Hampshire : Bauhan Publishing, 2025. |
Summary: "Marcy Rae Henry is the winner of the May Sarton New Hampshire Poetry Prize.
Identifiers: LCCN 2025020127 (print) | LCCN 2025020128 (ebook) | ISBN 9780872333987 paperback | ISBN 9780872333994 ebook
Subjects: LCGFT: Poetry
Classification: LCC PS3608.E5738 D43 2025 (print) | LCC PS3608.E5738 (ebook) | DDC 811/.6--dc23/eng/20250428
LC record available at https://lccn.loc.gov/2025020127
LC ebook record available at https://lccn.loc.gov/2025020128

For information on the May Sarton New Hampshire Poetry Prize: www.bauhanpublishing.com/may-sarton-prize/

Book design by Sarah Bauhan; typeset in Arno Pro
Cover design by Henry James using elements of a painting by marcy rae henry
Printed by Versa Press

marcy rae henry can be reached via her website
www.marcyraehenry.com

PO BOX 117 PETERBOROUGH NEW HAMPSHIRE 03458
603-567-4430
WWW.BAUHANPUBLISHING.COM

Follow us on Facebook and Instagram – @bauhanpub

MANUFACTURED IN THE UNITED STATES OF AMERICA

dedicada con mucho amor a mi abuelita Soledad Sosa

Contents

death is a mariachi

aspidoscelis neomexicanus (1)

a close-up of the desert floor
illuminated like the rest
by sun. we three, kings and all,
scatter like rain like whiptails
parthenogenetically reinventing
ourselves. in a desert
everything adapts.

body speech mind and action
a Tibetan sutra says
if you change genders
more than three times in a lifetime
it is an impediment to nirvana.

yoginis lie on a bed of light
a bed of nails
trying to slow down the heart.
the body takes care of itself
scarring over the way sidewalks
are repaired with more of themselves.

diurnal and in motion
whiptails do what they can to hide
means to survive.
it's a long shot.
red below, in the distance red
distinct from blue.
what if what happens on earth
stays on earth.

8th Day

—for Joy Michelle Tapia

My abuelo died when I was seven
Around that time my tío told me he didn't believe in God
I didn't know we had a choice

On some reservations
in New Mexico bodies
are placed directly into
the red earth
No boxes, coffins
or need to delay
the soul separating
from the skin
Wooden crosses
hammered into
the ground eventually
free themselves
Then they're stacked
in a big pile and no one
permanently marks the
earth

When a body is cremated
the heart burns slowly
Gold sublimates to gas
and travels up the chimney
Insects or fire reduce us all
to bone that has no need for adornment

When a body is cremated
teeth don't always burn
Bits of joints and jaw
remain
Sometimes a body's arms
lift up in the retort
As if reaching for a god
they hope believes in them

My first
high
school
boyfriend
died
recently
His
obituary
summed
him up
by saying
he liked
to fish
and
watch
crime
shows

Chile verde in my pueblo
points to the sun
which is undeniable
Eight days into death
blood decomposes
Similar to the chiles
the body starts changing
from green to red

The desert where I grew up
was filled with remnants of life
arrowheads, fossils, spines of animals
When I went to college in another desert
I briefly lived next to a crematorium
Who knows how many bodies
or how much gold I inhaled

At death the 'I' dies
leaving everyone reduced
to the third person singular
He/she/they with no voice
of their own
Buddhists spend a part
of every day preparing for it

aspidoscelis neomexicanus (2)

look closely—
as bluegreen tails swish
among red rocks

as whiptails scatter
a dark line between earth
and sky runs like mascara

lluvia en el desierto
para que podamos
continuar
golden oil in petrichor
used to be bottled in
India and put in perfume

look closely—
whiptails, always female, mating
swishing among rocks
cloning themselves
as if a prayer
of contagious words

the Buddha had no need
to distinguish between genders
all phenomena are inherently empty
a perfect purple breaking thru
the desert floor
the depression
light marking time

(Sonnet of sorts)

Horrible. I found a praying mantis in the bathroom. The insect that reminds me
of a particular ex who reminded me of the saddest violin. Before choking clouds,
before rain fell in sloppy splots, I tried my best to catch the mantis with a plastic bag.
Some things you want to release. Right after a dog walk the rain began. So humid I couldn't
eat. Some days it is enough to feed the dog, to unchoke. The mantis was missing one long
worshipful arm. What is a one-handed prayer? An uneven rain. What even is *I love you but*
only in motion. The mantis motioned to me to stop chasing him. I told him, I won't hurt you,
I will put you outside where it is bigger, greener. He wanted to know why I thought I knew
where he belonged. Why I couldn't just recognize he was a sign of wisdom and luck, patience
and perseverance, and let him be. Why I had to stop and research: do praying mantises bite
when I know very well everything bites. A flood warning flashed on my phone: *Most flood*
deaths occur in vehicles. Turn around, don't drown when encountering flooded roads.
Glad I didn't put the stick green insect outside; I still try to trap him in a poem
but really I think about him all night long and dry as kindling.

aspidoscelis neomexicanus (3)

the trouble in zazen
isn't you, baby, it's me
i am embodied
fe-male formed
and appendages
susceptible to lunar phases
and feminine phrases
sorry, but no
no, but
sorry
perhaps it is my karma

some mahayana sutras
say women can be
    enlightened
only not if female
a woman about to reach it—
nirvana—
will be reborn
as a man

how many lifetimes
have i spent
    in the wrong body
in the right body
but not in the mood
earth moon and sun
are in constant relation
the way we aged
under sheets was terrifying
which way did you go?
i wasn't done loving

this poem appears in

a nice day   a good price
          a sears catalog studied all night
     a changing room that makes you want to pee
as if the bar just closed   and you're walking home
knowing it's cold   but not feeling what you need to feel
 i say: i never understood what a training bra was for
     —train 'em for what?
 you say: you say the weirdest shit
at moments like this   and we walk home like gas
     elements   too far apart to find each other
          i feel the roots creeping under
   the stems transcending
what good does it do to look back
   on that time   when i had never read lispector
          before she had ever eaten lobster
     when i tied broken shoelaces together
               wrote by a bulb without a shade
walked in the rain   with my blood   all mixed up
   where they believed   my grandparents walked
          across the border when the truth is
they walked out of fields   finally   overcame
 the worst of the sun   pesticides   and everything else
     that finally planted them   in the ground
          like two native crops
     if only we had more than 1 – 10
to describe happiness,   sex,   last night's   thai food,
     pain,   panic,   teethgrinding   how badly
       you want to get home and fart   or stay home
     on christmas and just order thai food
a poem is born   in movement   stillness
 other people's shoes   in sickness and in stealth
          after all this time   i wonder
  how often we appear in each other

Architecture & Morality (1)

—after the third studio album by Orchestral Manoeuvres in the Dark (1981)

dead now all summer
the architecture of the tree is unbearable
everyone between borders has grown morally tired
whoever wrote *to be a flower is profound*
responsibility must have known
how tough it is to be a tree

while trying to remove an invasive plant with a root
two fingers thick like a moderate whiskey pour
shadows of birds circle the garden
i think of spring in San Luis Obispo
mamá and i calling it San Luis Obese
(it only works if you say Luis en español)

with Ávila Beach smeared in the distance
we walked through wooded hills toward a rafter
of wild turkeys (similar to the one that would surround
me when we lived in Monte Vista and i was unafraid)
as we got closer and they became vultures
mamá encouraged me to act alive
it's unbearable considering the things live people do

the tree did great
all the forest would be proud
it is covered in woodpecker xylem holes
that resemble *rat-a-tat-tat*
and remind me to look up who Coltrane
was thinking of when he wrote
'My one and only love'

i've always wanted to perform
my one love's only poem in English
the one who said if we amplified the frequency
of a space we could make it implode
the one whose face was like the tree outside
a house i had lived in a long time

(keep it back) til the ninth year

but first, just get to it said horace and i agree. talking about
the thing is not the thing itself. a meandering ars poetica
led me to look up *serpentinite*—a black olive, a wet golden
grape, the dark green gem before the necklace—source of
magnesium and asbestos. til today i hadn't thought of mining
for asbestos. i thought of avoiding it. house hunting and
standing beneath long white amosite asbestos–covered pipes
in a bungalow basement. mike telling me, you could get it
cleaned, but it would be expensive. telling mike how i'd ride
my bike by the building downtown in my hometown being
torn down and hold my breath as i pedaled by, imagining
dark needle-like fireproof fibers floating through the air.
some days i rode out to see flowers poking through the desert
floor while birds scattered like embers or ashes through
unfettered air. growing up i watched so many technicolor
movies, couldn't wait to get out into the world, find a place
that vibrant. now that they've dismantled the 500-pound
cameras that split images into three strips of film soaked
in cyan, magenta and yellow dye, i think of going home.
where there's no place to hide on the horizon and the freshly
mopped halfway houses are on one side of town and the bars
on the other. i never understood the holy ghost but i do believe
in recovery, in keeping the mouth clean. christmas being
the most wonderful time of the year. as a small brown child
i'd lie under our first silver tree while a tricolored pinwheel
lamp turned it into three different trees, deciding if red, green
or perhaps blue left me the happiest. maybe he didn't say
just get to it, but when he said don't let it out too soon,
what he really meant was hold your breath when you need to.

at the traffic light

you see street in line defining shape
light informing color. curved lines
make perfect circles around primary
and secondary hues. balance and im-
balance everywhere. vanishing points
in the distance. i see every lovable syllable.
three lines of haiku in ginsberg's american
sentence. if only i could stay in poetic mind
as if the root canal were the first snow.
you say *if only there was more nuance,*
the way some poet said something
enlightening somewhere. on piano F#
is the same as G♭. on violin they can be two
different sounds. not everyone can hear this
but that's not what you mean.
you want words where four thin lines
make a thick one. trompe-l'œil
of seven marks making a table for a platter
of emotions. if i could stay in poetic mind
until the light changes color, i would tell you:
in zazen to name something is to relinquish it.

consciousness seeks same

—after H. G. Wells's *The Island of Dr. Moreau*

sculpting is to add or subtract
is it easier to doctor beasts out of men
or make men out of torture?
the body is where it all begins
he divides us of ourselves
until it becomes impossible to recall which way we began
'not all living skin is painful' he insists
but the mind, helmeted by bone,
is inescapable and i need to be saved
come on, moreau! tell me of your god (invention or inter-
vention) tell me why i can't walk on all fours
or why i drank a sinful last night
while it rained like a telegraph typing out:
i won't come back for you   ever
everything needed to evolve is found in the sea
i can still taste it
the moment we emerged covered in sea foam
we breathed in fear
which can't be vivisected
and desire
which can't be grafted
the body remains in the mind
we're told it calls for meat and makeup
'i've never seen an animal think' he insists
but he doesn't know i've been considering living quietly
without cracking my gum
or swinging my axe
god has left us alone on the island
doing impressions of humans
having a bad day

deluge

older cousin, not by much. just enough.
'we have to give you the retarded test,'
she'd say when we were alone, forcing me
to answer questions and solve riddles.
she'd slur and mispronounce words
and might as well have been speaking farsi.
'fail!' she'd declare in a perfect pueblo accent.
'you're still retarded pues, pero no le cuentes
a nadie. it's supposed to be a secret.'

the direction of water in motion changes
depending on the hemisphere.
it's most noticeable when swirling around a drain.
not having one, an underpass in the pueblo
suddenly floods. just enough for a car to get stuck.
enough to trap someone in their car.
a guy swims through a downpour to save a stranger.
but how to fight against the heaviness of water?

she never fell in love, never learned to swim
and wouldn't get in a car with an equality sticker
because *she. wasn't. gay.*
she overestimated god, thinking she needed him
more than he needed her. but at that moment she
needed man.

oh, he pulled against nature and all her synonyms,
against the irony of drowning in the desert
against all reason—the reason behind
the search for a reason.
sometimes it all becomes breath,
becomes buddhist very quickly.
sometimes, to pull someone out
is to be pulled under.

let them eat light

it's an old story *women and children first*
when salt-eaten ships sank slowly
in international waters
settling down
barnacled and devoid of light
then hunted like treasure
or fugitives

children are dying
in Jimmy Santiago Baca's poem
metaphorical as *cider sunsets*
and *sombrero siestas*

children housed close to an imaginary line
drinking water out of imaginary toilets
the difference between fall and winter
is more than hardness   more than light

we come from the dead
die without papers or permission
we crawl heavy with bone   with shell
toward 'just having something'

carapace and plastron aren't hardened
in hatchlings
if we don't kill them first
we let the children die

news cameras slow-focus
children crossing
                    themselves

glowing with hope

Architecture & Morality (2)

—after the third studio album by Orchestral Manoeuvres in the Dark (1981)

wavering between feelings and places[1]
(structures in their own right)
is crucial
when to go means
take what you can carry
poetry in another language
a government with a history
of hating you, hating history
to stay, of course, is to sell sticky chiclets
on the street and nearly expired drinks
which means making ice
in all your pots and pans
dodging traffic and collecting glass
metal nearly expired food
across the raging city
it means not having toothpaste
at times tying broken shoelaces together
at times wavering
whether or not to go buy laces or paste
because no one has forgotten
who your father was

of course   you've no million dollars
to invest in another country
no chance to win the green card lottery
no blue eyes or yellow hair expected
by los Azteca on a man risen-from-death
who showed up riding a horse[2]

---

1. *a structure of feeling*
that's how metamodernists describe
a pendulum swinging
between modernism and postmodernism
a finger wagging
between seriousness and playfulness

2. metamodernists claim this era
of performatism integrates previous
and premodern sensibilities (which means
indigenous and traditional cultural codes)

no   for you the lines are long
the arrows drawn
you're the call of the wild
the long-lost child
coming or going
home
has mythological implications for you
beyond wood metal
            glass stone
it is feather bone black butterfly
a piece of obsidian
no buttresses to oblivion
it is line along horizon
and earth's contours
the opposite of owning rivers
and stars
it is sharing space
multiple names for place
the purpose of a temple
feng shui of planets
alignment with the four winds
and four directions
making a road around a meta-mountain
a metaphor out of a chore
less might've been more
before it was a bore
the page they tore out
about the Mother
—which ideology's less self
more other? what is our original purpose
and how do we function?

---

thank god 2020's hindsight
living it was a bitch

in China, a warning:
too much yin'll kill ya

who's your paperboy?
take the night off from knowing what you know

looking at a building won't change your life
but living in one will

memento mori

is why we're here
to glow in the dark
after the match burns out

to remember but speak not ill
of the dead   as if death
renders sin innocuous

a moth once flew into my mouth
i didn't know whether to spit
or swallow it whole
either way   the taste of dust for hours

the best letter of rejection
i ever got said: *we will not*
publish this poem as it is just
words describing other words

this country wants to win
perhaps a memento
on an IKEA shelf

mamá told us when 'taps'
is played at military funerals
the 24 notes come from a compu-
terized chip implanted in a bugle

the salutation of France's 17th century
hermits of St. Paul was *memento*
mori it is much more true
than *fine and you?*

The name of his body

Sure, I get what Bukowski is saying about the beer shit
but finishing a poem is stepping into a cathedral in a country
where your ancestors drank foot-stomped wine and prayed to leave.

When my cousin died, the cathedral wouldn't host his funeral.
Last thing that went through his mind was a bullet.
His was the first dead body I touched.

Before my love told me about Cioran: *writing about philosophy*
in another language is writing a love letter with a dictionary,
I looked up the word lesbian. I didn't get it, and philosophy didn't help.

I got my primo's story in bits y pedacitos. His wife had cheated.
Con una mujer. And he'd shot himself. Con su hijo a su lado en la cama.
Lesbian and suicide whispered as if saying syphilis.

In India I carried around two English dictionaries. Neither had good
translations for Moksha or Samsara. Had I known them at the time,
I would have wished my cousin escape from one, attainment of the other.

He was in uniform, his dark blue arm stiff as a salute.
What had he wanted? How would his son grow up with a lesbian?
How would he learn how to want?

Bukowski said *there is light somewhere* years after my cousin died.
Maybe he caught it on the way out. Would you prefer the gods
to delight in you or for you to delight in you?

promising a building is fireproof es como prometer amar pa' siempre

when los vecinos wake you
and you're half in sleep and half out
almost as if the moment before you fall in love
pero no tan bueno
and not at all like being half brown and half white
not even realizing til sitting on your abuelita's bed
and she touches your flat chest and says *tú tienes blanco in you*
not accusing not avoiding just informing
you of something no one on the street notices
and suddenly one summer she's fading failing
half in life means half out
and you feed her thru a plastic tube
trailing to her stomach and wonder how
it isn't un dolor sin final
but don't ask because to ask is to call attention
to tubes and a bit of whiteness
and dying makes her cold
así que no hay air con en el desierto
where if you stay late enough
you'll smell chile verde en tostadores
skins crackling at times charring
it's just the two of you all day
until mamá gets off work
so you walk around half naked
half the clothes required on the street
on the morphine clock your short-term memory starts to go
half remember half dream
and you sit next to your abuelita
sharing a moment of almost death intimate death
you crawl into bed with her the way you did as a child
when she tried to teach you prayers en español

but you were half in belief de un dios eterno   and half in fear
un fin de semana when you would normally be peeling skin
off chiles with her   sales a tomar una tequilita blanca
and you write a poem
in half light or half lit
and later it's only half as good as you think it is
you watch obama accept the nomination
your abuelita comes out of the morphine for a moment
the nurse comes once a day and you go for a bike ride
by an asbestos-filled building being knocked down
perhaps knocking asbestos everywhere
you ride by the arroyo or to the gym
to half remember your own body that can't possibly get old just forgotten
you come back to her rooms in the historic hotel
where 'fireproof' is painted at the back by the fire escape
you shower with the coldest water you can stand
and come out into stilted air
even a fan hurts her at this point
even a hug
you sit in your calzoncillos negros at the edge of her bed
so softly
so as not to remind her she's dying
she asks for more morphine
solo un poquito más
but won't say if it's for the pain of living or the pain of dying
you tell her *si le doy más you'll o.d.*
pero ya estoy dying anyway!
not on my watch you'll tell her
and regret it year after year
but for now you just sit on the edge of her bed
and she touches your clean hand then your bare chest

where a medallion would hang
and she teases *you have white in you*
as if someone poured it in drop by drop thru a feeding tube
plugged into la panza
not much   la verdad no mucho
más que yo she tells you

Architecture & Morality (3)

—after the third studio album by Orchestral Manoeuvres in the Dark (1981)

C was the last major chord
Chopin taught his students

not to flag Professor Cedrone
in 1981 everyone started with C

though i've never had it i know
i'm addicted to laudanum

i have what is known as motive
and a predilection for the color purple

in scales with black keys the middle finger
makes a bridge for the thumb to pass under

C major consists of all white keys
there's still debate about how to approach it

plug in an instrument made of wood
music needs no tuckpointing

Chopin has longevity even if he died at thirty-
nine coughing bloody roses into handkerchiefs

what C has going for it is that
it's the easiest to read

Music is a stimulant

He tells me sitting out back as if the tree in front wasn't dead.
He recently accepted five pillars, five prayers, five directions.
Movies, carnitas, mota… Abandoné también la música, he nods
at the speaker atop the table. Leaves gather beneath it.

Nos pregunta: Did you know Kadijah was fifteen years older
than the Prophet? As if a bendición. As if we didn't.
Cuando hablamos en español they're sure we're saying:
Meet me later in a room that needs an invitation.

At the top of the deck a moon, between hollow reeds cut to play
different notes in the breeze and 'Cruz de madera' filters through
the speaker. 'Una serenata por la madrugada.' *Do you want*
to be buried like Mozart o prefieres una tumba como Chopin?

I prefer a pine box to a mausoleum blinking like Vegas. And a cumbia
to a requiem. But really, I want to burn like trees. A danger to myself.
Clean as a Sacrament. Loud as a car alarm. No drum roll. No fade-out.
Go out in a minor key that suddenly turns major.

A ranchera comes on. Four-chord progression. Music is often math.
He taps my finger and we're holding onto each other atop a dead-wood deck
where, over my shoulder, his eyes go deep into my house. Like a splinter
in a finger that has been so many places. *It'll be hotter in there without*
the tree—he says to avoid saying: last call—*pero mucho más brillante.*

Architecture & Morality (4)

—after the third studio album by Orchestral Manoeuvres in the Dark (1981)

for Professor Frank Cedrone

it is the Electronic Age
same as it was in the '40s

i heard robot pop a decade after it debuted
and it sounded fresh to me

someone i met by chance
reminded me of everything

i remember the small blue hardback books
that claimed pioneers settled the Borderlands

sometimes you're born with perfect pitch
sometimes you need to pass a test

Professor Cedrone said if i mastered the masters
i could play electronica with my elbow

he taught me what his teacher taught him about
competing: place a stone in your left shoe

the brain will be too occupied with left/right hand
sustain pedal and pebble to focus on nervousness

it's good to be behind the altar instead of atop it
to feel stones in shoes instead of around the neck

there are still instruments that need breath
still time to meet someone else

i have always lived here

this field of mint, crushed by desire
those who question what they deserve

every year latitude
and longitude humping in the storm
for something greener

every year finding a way
to call something love

i have lived here rearranging pictures
on the wall to see them again

here is where i've lived
a world lacerated with field
song rows of dead below living

*

abuelita planted first—
my mother—
i really had no choice

when the Depression
she quit school to top bloody beets
beneath a toothache of sun

here is where going to the well
is simply about water

when the depression
—a decrescendo
descending

*

here is when light hurts
jostling the birds

dry eyes keep me from
seeing through ignorance

i read green is only visible on earth
not having been elsewhere ...

i suffer fields of mint
finding a way to love someplace

North of the Pearl River in Canton *(every time i look ahead it all looks north to me)*

the Peasant Movement Institute is north of the Pearl River

Ios is north of Oia and Paros is north of Ios

Oscar Wilde's bones are north in The Cimetière du Père Lachaise

Amadeo Modigliani
remains below Wilde

to the east
is Chopin's grave

Shwezigon
Pagoda
golden as
the Punjabi
temple
as golden
as basílicas
in Spain

oily ports in Portugal

warm water in Maho Bay

Pokhara below Machhapuchhare

cold caves in Manila

sacred dirt in Chimayó

hydrofoils Algeciras to Tangier

(the mind pulls up the cities of the world for a compass)

in Uttar Pradesh Muslims pray facing west El Volcán Sumaco is southeast of Quito

ruins of the Ottoman rival those of Roma

Aleppo has been continuously inhabited longer than almost every other city

Naddi is
west of
Dharamsala
and west
of Naddi
is the sunset

Avenue Anywhere

A
change
of scenery

for the eternal
internal struggle

Las Sandia
mountains are
watermelon
colored at dusk
and sit east of
Albuquerque

Travertine terraces in Turkey

Western Wall in the Temple Mount

the Reeperbahn of Hamburg runs east and west

Temples in Beijing *(like heaven and hell)* built along a north
south axis [facing south]

the Tivoli
in southwest
Copenhagen

between Africa and
Asia—Aqaba—in
southernmost Jordan

← Wacker Dr. follows a river whose flow was reversed →

Wacker Dr. runs ✥ north south east west

(the mind forgets all the places the body has been)

Pizzerias in every direction in Paris in Venice water everywhere

2 a.m. Canada's fires raging (too tired to look for a cough drop)

my dog and i vying for center of the bed
spines pressed together
the fan doesn't drown out birds
who've found something to sing about
in skies of smoke
no W for Chicago
though we made it to the top
of the world's worst air quality
the mind pulls up cities of the world
hazy temples in Delhi and Beijing
collars gray from smog
blowing into a hanky and soot coming out
the ex-boyfriend who fought forest fires
blew sooty snot for days after a bonfire gone bad
said everything he ate tasted burnt
tortillas are the only things that taste good burnt
but he couldn't just eat torts

though i can't see them i feel my eyes
red as if i stepped off a red-eye
Beijing, Lima, Kathmandu, Delhi
places the mind forgets
the body remembers
throat sore from just air
lying linked spines with the dog
who doesn't understand why we can't go to the park
when the world smells like burnt bark
bbq or flames vying for the center
throat drier than after a night of hookah
too tired to get up and look for a cough drop
i was sure sat atop the nightstand
too busy trying to sleep
trying not to single out a birdsong
or pick out the sound of a train

the cough drops are full of sugar anyway
Luden's—
bought because they were sold in the desert
in rectangular boxes
red oblong lozenges and we pretended to be sick
because they tasted the same as cherry candy
how much opium was used in cough syrup
cocaine for toothaches
how much cough syrup
to escape the confines of a mind
circumstances of a bed in a house
in a city close to Canada filled with smoke

gravity (fundamental interaction causing mutual attraction between things that have mass)

you stand in black
while i sit
like a stone heap
at the edge of the freshwater
lake filled with rain
the reversed flow of the river
carried typhoid and cholera
toward the mississippi
remnants of tanned
leather and barges
transporting hides of animals
heavy with dye
the stench of blood
and fear of death

chicago smells awful
when it needs a good rain
to carry sewage
to purification plants
there is talk about restoring the river
to its natural course
for now i sit marooned
as if our ship has sailed
or is sailing
you all in black
twiddling a necklace
bouncing back and forth
like a postmodern poem
between aging eyes
and shiny jewelry

it's three ice cubes a week
i tell you about overwatering

my money tree
drilling holes in the bottom
of the plastic pot
soil from home depot
that isn't truly soil

fog mocks the sunset
i sit transfixed
squinting up
as if to say yes
as if to blur you
into the horizon
the platform on which
to perform a ritual

startling sounds
crack and pop
through July's sun-shot sky
it pauses the beach
puts us in each other's eyes

birds scatter
singing hallelujahs
colors fall
like a handful of spiders
into the lake
you hold out your hand
i try not to stand too quickly
you aren't loud enough yet

Talking pictures

The desert is more of a listener
Not the uncourageous kind
More of a Socratic type
When Edward Abbey said the most spiritual thing
About the desert is it doesn't give a shit
That's not what he meant
As any barber will tell you: there's more
To the story
And stories are one of the few things
That take the sting out of death
Try asking someone who fancies themself
A philosopher why those homies
Were in Plato's cave in the first place
They'll tell you you're missing the point
But why'd they go into the fuckin cave? is as good
A question as any and better than:
How many points is this worth?
Refraining from lying is not the same as
Oh, you already know this
But let me tell you: Very few rumors
In the desert
That's why it kicks you in the ass
It has all the access
The way conquistadores had access
To more than our philosophy
And I know that to call it that retroactively
Lends a self-consciousness
That wasn't there before
I'm also looking for a sustainable burial
To hell with forever

flashback

you won't speak to me
from far, far away

one of my cousins
made me eat dirt

at least we were in
the mountains not the city

his sister and i used a stick
to poke the eyes out of a dead fish

these two things i forgot
to tell you

when chaplin fell
people laughed

but that kinda thing
isn't funny anymore

She needs to know my skin isn't whitening but my hair is

It scares me to have my lists taken away

Wax
Stamps
Parchment

When I stay awake in the blackness
squinting myopically on my side of the border
I challenge myself to write letters to Z
and seal them in envelopes before I regret them

wolves cooperate on the kill
they can follow a scent across
the Río Grande

In the letters I ask her to bring me things I need in the desert
and draw crude maps where the road forks in my direction
but I don't ask when she will return

Thread
Turmeric
Tulips

She needs to know I am brown but not embarrassed
I am naked at least twice each day   I just have to remind myself
to stop dying
in the feminine way   and to buy more things

Whetstone
Oil
Lemons
Linen

While the wax is drying I write different endings to our story
They always include the ceremony she suggested
where we lick bee syrup off each other's fingers

And just when I make progress
I erase and start over (pressing on the pencil
so the indentations will still be available)

in a wolfpack
only the dominant
male and female breed

No question who would be top dog were Z and I wolves
She is monotheistic foreign but exotic
So she can come and go as she pleases

At times it pleases her not to respond
Or to ignore my need for

Matches
Kindling
Kissing

When she lived with me she'd wake at halfday and walk through
the living room halfnaked her tips poking at her t-shirt
implying flight at any moment

She would bring me sunflowers
And toss my enumerations into a bin
filled with ground coffee and piles of peels and rinds

The victors gave us a saint and a prayer for lost things
Hard to say if she is lost or just gone
But if they keep bringing us old-world diseases wrapped in blankets

and plastic and setting the dogs on us   I'll have to keep
shifting south and she might never find me

even a lone wolf seeks out another wolf
because wolves want
to belong to each other

If Z comes back she'll have to be transparent
as a palimpsest   and stop washing me off her
Then we can update the guest list
and buy things to hold a ritual

Censer
Silver rings
Hair dye

(pueblo has a piece of guadalupe hidalgo on display)

christmas is the time for asking
(and iconography)
light was moving forward before becoming color
we couldn't have continued with all this paper
(no one has reclaimed *bastard*)
we need a middleman to receive god's forgiveness
(maybe it's a matter of semantics)
borders are lines on a curving earth
perspective is the earth as another dot
dot dot is morse code for the line and dot known as 'i'
(yo is not capitalized en español)
what were we to learn in that building
(every poem is a found poem)

dream life of night owls

it's easy to learn three chords on the guitar
and sing about the world
as if it's carried around in a pink paper
bag and forgotten on the train.

i am never drunk in dreams.
in my head, as if a foot too big for a shoe,
i am the age i was when i fell asleep.
and i can improvise jazz stops.

forward as far as i've lived. and backward
to polyester, to peeing into pants because scary
white santa picked me up with thin white gloves
the way librarians pick up Mayan manuscripts.

they wrote about dreams with language reserved
for myths and stories. about ceiba trees upholding
a world soft and pink in spots. and roots creeping
down to the underworld.

in a dream i never look into a mirror.
and i don't tell anyone i am time-traveling.
a three-chord song plays in the background.
and i am very careful about how i dance.

in a dream, on a train, my love made promises
and i carried them around as if they were
carefully painted on vellum. she made myth
of everything. and i believed.

the sound of phantom trains keeps me up at night.
night eyes blink on a tree.
while awake i tell no one i know how to fly.
it's like having a mistress.

el molcajete

before los conquistadores arrived and dropped off the cross and we picked up the guilt and saints started to trend, we were holding onto an aguacate-shaped tejolote. estabamos moliendo, grinding, crushing ajo, chile, cebolla in a three-legged stone molcajete. pedacitos stuck to the stone making abuelita's guacamole taste slightly different, slightly better than anyone else's. as a child i thought molcajete y tejolote were 'mortar and pistol' en inglés. kind of like thinking 'Silent Night' went ... *round yon virgin mother and child, holy infant, so tender and wild*... when i discovered the original Nahuatl words *molcaxitl* and *texolotl*, i had a hard time saying them. kind of the way we have a hard time saying goodbye when we know someone is dying.

el molcajete was used by los aztecas y los mayas, whom some say they subjugated before conquistadores arrived with guns and horses and complicated the rest of the story with their voracity. not completely unlike familias who Christmas together but don't always get along and sometimes get worse when someone is dying, starting arguments that begin with, *that's mine; yo quiero ésto*. abuelita's molcajete was cured long ago, between la revolución mexicana and men on the moon, by grinding arroz grain by grain until there were no black basalt bits to wear down the teeth. it sat unused all summer, garlic, chile and onion stuck to the stone, that summer when we listened to 'Suavecito' by Malo as if por primera vez. that summer when kids jumped in and out of the fountain on Grand Ave. before the old jail was turned into a hotel and a bar with free breadsticks. the summer we used abuelita's small marble molcajete to grind pills into powder to pass through a tube into her stomach to numb the pain of life burning up.

molcajetes can be put over coals to cook something and afterwards, esa comida will stay hot a long time. molcajetes de mármol son fácil limpiar. but to clean a stone molcaxitl, brush the stone and rinse it well. never use soap because if it sticks to la piedra puede aparecer en la salsa, tasting bad as cilantro. as basalt is ground down it rejuvenates itself, so molcajetes can last a long time. but there is no cure for what abuelita has, no wearing down the black bits, no rejuvenating, regenerating. every night is a silent night, a holy night. la mañana un milagro.

ese verano abuelita's voice got gravelly as Chavela's, and when she sang, she really sang, and when she sang it sounded like bits of molcajete stuck to her throat. she started to see people who were visiting from heavenly realms. *glories stream from heaven afar.* some days she was closer to them than to me. ese verano every day crushing those pills as if days or dreams while abuelita watched the clock expectantly as a celibate beneath the cross. *heavenly hosts sing alleluia.* cada día crush, grind, crush, grind. pastillas pulverized to dust that doesn't stick to marble. pills to the tube. pills to the pestle. someone called dibs on the small gray molcajete while we were still using it to keep her alive. or to keep her from the pain of living. *christ the savior is born!* tejolote to pastilla to molcajete. machacar, triturar, moler. someone took el rosario que le llevé de la Catedral Metropolitana de la Ciudad de México. kind of like carting off golden stones to erect a monument across the ocean. *all is calm. all is bright.* sometimes molcajetes have animal faces or designs on them. *radiant beams from thy holy face.* a veces, colores. *with the dawn of redeeming grace.* unos molcajetes antiguos had lids. these were used in the burial of important members of society. *sleep in heavenly pea-ce. slee-eep in heavenly peace.*

Contemporary Compass Rose

(1300 → 2008)

North

Northern lights: beautiful colorful collision
Gets colder the farther you go
You can get there by going northwest
'Get back to where you once belonged'
The Great Migration
¡Pa'l norte!
¡América!
¿Canadá ?

Pacific Northwest
Cascadia totem poles 100 days of rain
Postmaster thought NM was in Old
México

Nor'easter
Unlike Miller 'Type B'
Miller 'Type A' starts in the
Midwest

West

Used to be called The Occident
(sounds like accident with an accent)
Christians
Capitalismo
Historically anti-Communist
'West end town dead end world'
More sparsely populated than *back east*
The west as in: Cowboys

East

Used to be called The Orient
Orient yourself by the north star
and turn right to go east
En español todavía es el oriente
así que give mamá un break
Often referred to as *back east* as in:
going *back east* even if you've never been
The East as in: Indians

Aztlán
Borderlands
Unparalleled beauty
Under siege

U.S. slave settlements
Humid subtropical climates on
the southeast side of nearly all
continents

South

Belles made minty juleps
(not mojitos) while Americans fought
to keep people enslaved
South of the border: from where Vicente Fox
lectured the U.S. on gun control
A great place to vacation
According to the media: gets more dangerous the farther you go

a game to see who says i love you first

it's still early in the season but i say prayers i haven't said in years
in so long i question why i stopped saying them
because now they sound strange and magical in the mouth
and ~~my mouth~~ god feels strange in my mouth

you used to choose all my titles
before the absence of ~~you~~ god came leaking out
at the most inconvenient times
you used to write your name over mine

i know it's mostly chemicals
but ~~laundry soap~~ a sacrament smells clean all the same
words are useful as bones
i use them to keep ~~you~~ god in my mouth

you have difficulty dealing with time in the usual way
separating it from space, thinking it's not physical
god will always be there
behaving as if ~~god~~ i will always be there

if the maya played a game

trying to get a ball
through a stone hoop
or trying to keep
the ball in the air
perhaps reenacting the creation
myth or keeping the sun
and moon in their orbits and if
sometimes the losing team
would be executed (at times
the winning group as well)
it was ritual to the gods
we create one every day
every day we do it to be loved
we wave our arms at the sky
as if someone were watching
we line up to glimpse dead kings
marvel at peopling
crowding coupling
separating
drafting up exams
instruments of pleasure
music
torture
looking for a place to sleep
on dry land
toddling at times
teetotaling
i forgot to add—some games
were meant to settle disputes
with a rubber ball
instead of waging war
i forgot footnotes of
goodevil deathlife
herotwins and some games
played for fun

what do we mean
when we say
be a sport
when we wash habitually
eat chocolate
use the zero
wait
trim hair
record events
sculpt carve
paint decorate
mold narrate
battle axing
conceiving
sacrificing
front line lives
in the name of
avoiding death

last payphone in times square

she came up to my eye.
i asked to borrow a pen.

people attend the removal of the
last payphone in times square.

i wrote her number in a note-
book stained into lines.

a power saw is used for the phone.
eulogies are said.

first time i called
set something in motion.

no one finds panegyrics to public
payphones unusual.

in my space we traded sketches.
hunger can be a project.

no one carries coins in pockets.
coins are an insult.

strawberries rotted in the fridge.
we woke each other up.

the fate of the phone is unknown.
museums have the best storage.

she gave me a piece of raw amber.
pine leather scents still intoxicate.

the last call was cinematic.
the end. as hollywood calls it.

the mammal that has the longest orgasm

first thing to do before moving is to take stock
toss socks, eat all the food and light as many fires
as you can because you may not have another fireplace
and because burning is more fun than shredding

midwestern wood, wet and aging like cheese,
takes forever to light but my last apartment
in albuquerque caught fire without anyone trying

first thing to do before moving in with someone
is not to talk about sums or money or psalms
we slept together before living together—and after—
everything in between was fights and fondue
every night with O. was counting black sheep

with orgasms between 30 and 90 minutes
the sus scrofa domesticus is not just any pig
O. claimed that if someone had a 30-minute orgasm
they'd want to commit suicide afterwards

now, moving means i put the sky in a box
countless pairs of sight and sun glasses
then a model of the city where nothing looks dangerous
i put mirrors in a box
pink salt lamps
a gramophone O. gifted me on my 30th birthday
and my great-grandparents' naturalization papers

too many euphemisms for death
the mammal with the longest orgasm
is not necessarily the happiest
in the echo of empty walls painted white
i light a cigarette just to have something burning

you could be the lake

places in my house
i want to take you

afternoon light beaming in the center
of prosecco rings on my dresser

palm prints on the headboard
moon pulling us inside out

the lake eats everything
not everything is digestible

you could be the lake
or you could be everything

something chest-level or top floor
or top shelf has me dumbstruck

water is a mystery
in all forms

you paused at my bookshelves
fingering orange spines

though not to scale a tired map
contains the places we're from

you move like a day across the week
i'm drawn to blue around the world

we could go out tonight
or stand here under lights forever

flowers tangling
planes flying in and out

unless one of us starts
the other can't let go

what to do with shriveling apples

into boxes pewter candlestick holders
red wax over white wax over black
boxes of letters in blue cursive
belts of various sizes
books carried in one by one
readied to be carried out

you can still hang up on people
but what to do with first publications of old lovers
extra hairbrushes and shriveled apples
all i really need are my screwdrivers
sports bras and yoga mats

in India i lived out of a rucksack for years
trading books with others
makeshift altars
what i missed most was not perfume but salt

boxes remind me of my back
being in love isn't always being heavy with future
boxes are a sign of attachment
and therefore not very Buddhist

empty boxes not as fun as emptying
cardboard is strong but not like a boxer
you can't practice being alone
can't trust people to go to their corners

yes and maybe go into a box—
poems into a box
words into a poem
orchards and shade and different hues of red
Cézanne said — 'Be an apple!'
to his portrait sitters
and they just sat there

real feel 109

the real feel in chicago is 109
it is the experience of heat
makes me temper myself around you

my father used to run a beer mug under
the faucet before sticking it in the freezer
the first touch on frost left fingerprints

you are like the first night
sleeping in a new room
every time i see you
    one of us is taller than the other

after college i lived in a spanish attic
and two places in india without refrigeration

my father was the type of guy
who would say: *he's the type of guy*
who'd complain if his ice was cold

we are abstract in the dark
a mosaic of yellow tiles floating out like bees
    almost a dead cow in water

i want to practice with you but it's no use
if i were a percentage i'd be halfway charged

in its solid state water can be held in the hand
but the experience of you lacks the real feel of you
if drained of blood the heart appears white

still life

in a world lit first by flame
then by spark
apple once referred to nuts
and fruit that wasn't berries
tomatoes were once love apples
the way potatoes are earth apples
devil's trumpets are thorn apples
oranges chinese apples

a knife twists
halves and quarters
you need one person to tell you
it's going to be alright
even if it's splitting apart

when more horses than cars
traversed this city birds sang
the same songs they do today
outside the window
of our melancholy world
where we create names for fruit
for fights for fancy

after apples
pears are most nutritious
they model good behavior
obey laws of gravity
we take for granted
they may not relieve each
other's boredom
but like neighbors
make the most of
the time and space
they're granted

Prozac makes its debut

On Sunday we agree it will be 1987 all day
even when we change the subject. A key
to a door that once opened to a garden.
The longing to pull the fire alarm. Driving home
a terrible parable. The record player moves
in a circle not a line. Lines on our faces
are mistakes. Classical continuity when a jump
cut would do. Bands like racehorses. Some
like big fat houses. It is not recall. Not regret.
It is small zesty shavings. Dancing on toes
when the soles will do. When holding hands
meant something. Beautiful and insubstantial
as a crowning meringue. Everything behind us
is in front. A decade of sunrise.
We were all unknown. Practiced drums to
radios and acid rain. Built Thursday
as if failing a test. All day we believe aliens
might save us. We wait for '87 to kick in,
for something to restore our interest in daily living.

hera's western grove

the youth of you
unravels from the you of you
slips out from the narrow
sidestreet throat of you
i follow your skin
tight as apples
into a dream
where i fall
    and fall
        fall until
jerking awake
in another dream
in eden's garden
the fruit remained unnamed
could have been blue
purple orange soft seedless
poisonous hallucinogenic
remained generic
a loanword a melon
simply *tree fruit*
had the movement
the maintenance of the hesperides
not added red delicious to the story
    i say all this under the influence
of the pain of wanting pleasure
the story i want to get out
before it gets loose

*a 3.2-mile path of 110-mile-per-hour winds**

when the storm knocked the electricity out
i ran to 7-eleven to get ice and placed chile verde
in coolers as if in a tabernacle.

people drove on sidewalks because hundred-year-old
trees choked the streets. on clean paper
i wrote: *things to do when you're not in love...*

the silence of having but not having washing machines
and water heaters hung around
like ice in January. night after night stars prevailed.

chiles that didn't fit in coolers defrosted in a pool
of cool green water.
in a pandemic the barrio is everything.

i charged my phone in the truck and read: *a twister*
touched down in Chicago...people rented
U-Hauls, pried open stores and took what they wanted.

trees crushed roofs and windshields. electrical wires
hung like vines, hid like snakes.
a neighbor and i mapped out a route for the dogs.

mamá no recuerda el clima
cuando yo nací. i've forgotten the darkness
and light inside her.

summer before last we raced flames and smoke
through mountains, through La Veta Pass before it became
unpassable. las fotos son lindas. absent of fear.

weeks later i drove from Borderlands to Chicago
con chile verde or mira soles or 'sunlookers'
frozen in coolers.

after the storm the neighbor made lemon garlic kale salad.
i cooked chiles en salsa de tomate, toasted tortillas.
and we ate at separate ends of a wooden deck.

*Five tornadoes touched down in the Chicago area on August 10, 2020.

where lines go (please hold)

i look to you to see where lines on my face will go
knowing i smoked hookah and opium
drank at times instead of breathing deep
thought up a character who thought an innovative
way to die would be to knock a rusted railroad spike
found on the side of the tracks straight into the chest
—out, damned heart, out

do you categorize the morning-after pill
as aborting or avoiding
know that planned parenthood mailed out
the daily pill for free when i was in college
now i say heat when i mean cool
in heat
in a different kind than before
the kind that belongs in a ski resort
i like the idea of moderation
forget the word for can opener in English
and estrógeno in Spanish

i look to you to change what i can—
lighten here darken there
a strange night, before i'd ever been to New Orleans
to march in a second line,
because, you know, i wanna be in that number,
one of us called the hotline for help
the person who answered said:
suicide prevention, please hold…
one of us thought it the funniest thing they ever heard
and got back in line

unfinished/the Taos hum

when orange has been
smashed to shit
pulverized to sticky
pummeled so much it turns yellow—
that is the color, my synesthetic friend says.

have you ever heard the 'Taos hum'?
i ask. *it could be aliens or mind*
control. it could drive you mad.

someone whispers, *it looks unfinished...*
in front of an Agnes Martin painting,
like an embarrassed public prayer.
cloudy blue barely distinguishable
from white.

you wouldn't remember it.
you probably didn't notice how,
like Martin's lines, we almost touched,
almost became visible to each other.

not everyone hears 'the hum.'
some are hearers and some are listeners.
my friend said he could make a portrait of us
looking as if 'little work was put in.'

polygraph of the amnesiac

i tell you there are 5 black doors in front of me
and i want to paint one red.

amnesia is typically violent.
non-penetrating business is common
and reasonably understood.

the brain suffers playback. non-
penetrating violent failure.

don't scrimp recreating the crime
in the shittiest room of a motel 8.
cut her toenails a little too close.

the picture in the 4th hallway is of a real
king but the painting next to it is fake.

time starts behind every door.
light moves across walls, self-reflective.
a mosquito buzzes in F#.

confabulation takes over where heaven ends.
a lie disguised as déjà vu.

we are what fills in gaps in god's memory.
the cafeteria line moves in a fugue state.
choose any soup, warm or cold.

desire, unlike color, is not remembered.
no chance of reoffending.

start with looking

and because i feel gutted like a fish free of bones
no longer knitted together by skin and scale

and because the most peaceful i ever felt was living alone
in a monk's hut in the middle of India with panthers crawling
through early morning light as sun cleared the mountain of guilt

and because i can't seem to reach you with brown fingers
snaked with veins undeniably full of themselves

and because it's not the right time of night or i don't have the right
rhyme or shyness gets stuck in the throat like a bone

and because ceroid cacti only bloom once a year for just one night

and because all the words i owe you are stacked like books,
like boxes, blocks and cans of food

and because you remind me of an earth held together
by magic and magnetic poles

and because you never get stage fright while i'm waiting
for the curtain to go up and a spotlight to cover us in shine

and because i got robbed on a train traveling through India
but still ride trains all the time

and because a fire in the fall smells as perfect as petrichor

and because some of my belongings were stolen at a Buddhist center
in Burma where i took vows of no killing no stealing no lying no
sexual conduct and knew there was so much i could do without

and because the antidote for feeling gutted is feeling grateful

and because in India i ate anything fried and soaking in syrup
i can imagine thighs in the game of cause and effect

and because no flag exists that would explain how i feel

and because only when i die can i say i had the time of my life

Acknowledgments

Thank you to the following presses and journals for publishing earlier versions of these pieces, and to Steven Alvarez for selecting *Dream Life of Night Owls* as winner of the Open Country Poetry Chapbook Contest.

BathHouse: *Contemporary Compass Rose, North of the Pearl River in Canton*

Best New Poets 2023 Anthology: *last payphone in times square*

carte blanche: *a 3.2-mile path of 110-mile-per-hour winds*

Cherry Tree: *let them eat light, memento mori*

The Columbia Review: *promising a building is fireproof es como prometer amar pa' siempre*

The Dewdrop: *start with looking*

DoubleCross Press: *Contemporary Compass Rose, 8th Day, flashback, North of the Pearl River in Canton, She needs to know my skin isn't whitening but my hair is*

epiphany: *She needs to know my skin isn't whitening but my hair is*

Hobart: *flashback*

Lumiere: JUSTICE initiative*:* *polygraph of the amnesiac*

Moon City Review: *the mammal that has the longest orgasm*

Mud Season Review: *consciousness seeks same, last payphone in times square, real feel 109*

Open Country Press: *aspidoscelis neomexicanus (1), aspidoscelis neomexicanus (2), dream life of night owls, gravity (fundamental interaction causing mutual attraction between things that have mass), (keep it back) til the ninth year, last payphone in times square, let them eat light, the mammal that has the longest orgasm, Molcajete, (Sonnet of sorts), Music is a stimulant, The name of his body, polygraph of the amnesiac, promising a building is fireproof es como prometer amar pa' siempre, (pueblo has a piece of guadalupe hidalgo on display), 2 a.m. Canada's fires raging (too tired to look for a cough drop), what to do with shriveling apples, where lines go (please hold)*

Oyster River Pages: *unfinished/the Taos hum*

Pangyrus: *8th Day*

RHINO: *Molcajete*

Rough Cut Press: *Music is a stimulant*

Salamander: *if the maya played a game, this poem appears in*

The Shore: *Prozac makes its debut*

So to Speak: *dream life of night owls*

Sunspot Lit: *you could be the lake*

The Worcester Review: *a game to see who says i love you first*

Heartfelt thanks to: mamo, Gini Henry, Chaco, mis abuelitos, the crash at *RHINO Poetry*, with extra gracias to Virginia Bell and Sarah Jack, Jen Karmin, Anne Yoder, Poppy Brandes, Heather McShane, Ron Falzone, Martha Soriano, Marina Merli, Yolanda Nieves, Natalie Peeterse, Emily Perkovich and everyone at Querencia Press, Diego Báez, Germán, Sarah Bauhan, Dorsey Craft Olbrich, and, of course, May Sarton.

The May Sarton New Hampshire Poetry Prize

The May Sarton New Hampshire Poetry Prize is named for May Sarton, the renowned novelist, memoirist, poet, and feminist (1912–1995) who lived for many years in Nelson, New Hampshire, not far from Peterborough, home of William L. Bauhan Publishing. In 1967, she approached Bauhan and asked him to publish her book of poetry, *As Does New Hampshire*. She wrote the collection to celebrate the bicentennial of Nelson, and dedicated it to the residents of the town.

May Sarton was a prolific writer of poetry, novels, and perhaps what she is best known for—nonfiction on growing older (*Recovering: A Journal*, *Journal of Solitude*, among others). She considered herself a poet first, though, and in honor of that and to celebrate the centenary of her birth in 2012, Sarah Bauhan, who inherited her father's small publishing company, launched the prize. (www.bauhanpublishing.com/may-sarton-prize)

PAST MAY SARTON WINNERS:

In *The Wreck of Birds,* the first winner of Bauhan Publishing's May Sarton New Hampshire Poetry Prize, Rebecca Givens Rolland embraces an assimilation of internal feeling and thought with circumstances of the natural world and the conflicts and triumphs of our human endeavors. Here, we discover a language that seeks to at once replicate and transcend experiences of loss and disaster, and together with the poet "we hope that such bold fates will not forget us." Even at the speaker's most vulnerable moments, when "Each word we'd spoken / scowls back, mirrored in barrels of wind" these personal poems insist on renewal. With daring honesty and formal skill, *The Wreck of Birds* achieves a revelatory otherness—what Keats called the "soul-making task" of poetry.

—Walter E. Butts, New Hampshire Poet Laureate (2009–2013), and author of *Cathedral of Nervous Horses: New and Selected Poems,* and *Sunday Evening at the Stardust Café*

Rebecca Givens Rolland is a speech-language pathologist and doctoral student at the Harvard Graduate School of Education. Her poetry has previously appeared in journals including *Colorado Review, American Letters & Commentary, Denver Quarterly, Witness, and the Cincinnati Review,* and she is the recipient of the Andrew W. Mellon Fellowship, the Clapp Fellowship from Yale University, an Academy of American Poets Prize, and the Dana Award.

Nils Michals won the second May Sarton New Hampshire Poetry Prize in 2012, and has also written the book *Lure*, which won the Lena-Miles Wever Todd award in 2004. His poetry has been featured in *The Bacon Review*, *diode*, *White Whale Review*, *Bay Poetics*, *The Laurel Review* and *Sonora Review*. He lives in Santa Cruz, California and teaches at West Valley College.

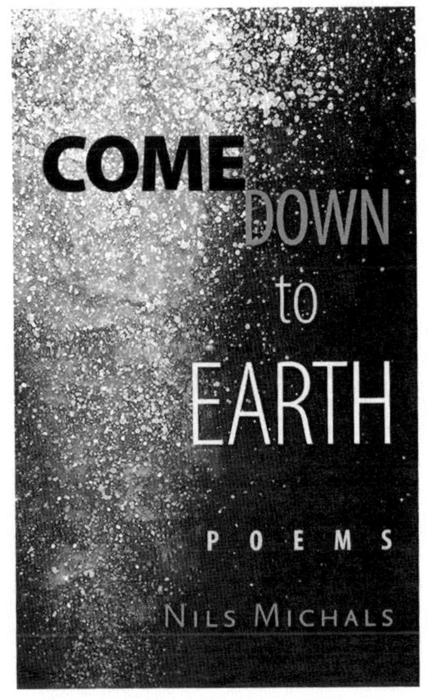

Nils Michals is alternately healed and wounded by the tension between the timeless machinations of humankind and the modern machinery that lifts us beyond—and plunges us back to—our all-too-human, earthly selves. Supported by minimally narrative, page-oriented forms, his poems transcribe poetry's intangibles—love, loss, hope, a sense of the holy—in a language located somewhere between devotional and raw, but they mourn and celebrate as much of what is surreal in today's news as of what is familiar in the universal mysteries . . . *Come Down to Earth* is a 'long villa with every door thrown open' "

—Alice B. Fogel, New Hampshire Poet Laureate (2014-2019), and author of *Strange Terrain: A Poetry Handbook for The Reluctant Reader* and *Be That Empty*

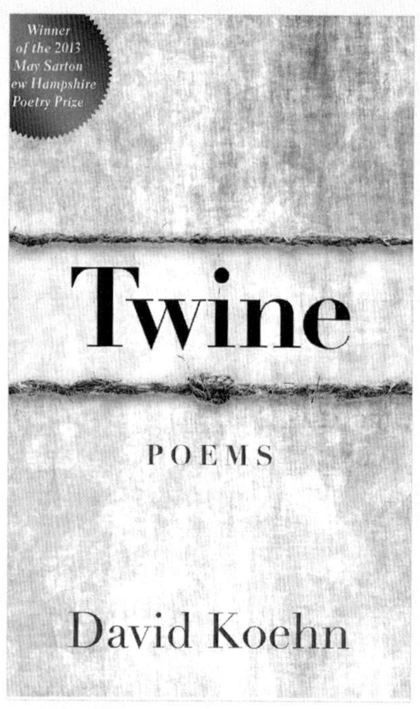

David Koehn won the third May Sarton New Hampshire Poetry Prize in 2013. His poetry and translations were previously collected in two chapbooks, *Tunic,* (speCt! books 2013) a small collection of some of his translations of *Catullus,* and *Coil* (University of Alaska, 1998), winner of the Midnight Sun Chapbook Contest. He lives with his family in Pleasanton, California.

David Koehn's first book, *Twine,* never falters—one strong poem after another. This is the work of a mature poet. His use of detail is not only precise and evocative; it's transformative."

—JEFF FRIEDMAN, 2013 May Sarton New Hampshire Poetry Prize judge and author of *Pretenders*

David Koehn's imagination, rambunctious and abundant, keeps its footing: a sense of balance like his description of fishing: "Feeling the weight . . . of the measurement of air." That sense of weight and air, rhythm and fact, the ethereal and the brutal, animates images like boxers of the bare-fist era: "Hippo-bellied/And bitter, bulbous in their bestiary masks." An original and distinctively musical poet.

—ROBERT PINSKY,
United States Poet Laureate, 1997-2000 and author of *Selected Poems,* among numerous other collections

Deborah Gorlin won the 2014 May Sarton New Hampshire Poetry Prize. She has published in *Poetry, Antioch Review, American Poetry Review, Seneca Review, The Massachusetts Review, The Harvard Review, Green Mountains Review, Bomb, Connecticut Review, Women's Review of Books, New England Review,* and *Best Spiritual Writing 2000.* Gorlin also won the 1996 White Pine Poetry Press Prize for her first book of poems, *Bodily Course.* She holds an MFA from the University of California/Irvine. Since 1991, she has taught writing at Hampshire College, where she serves as co-director of the Writing Program. She is currently a poetry editor at *The Massachusetts Review.*

In poem after poem in *Life of the Garment,* Deborah Gorlin clothes us in her fabric of sung words, with characters unique and familiar, and facsimiles of love that open and close their eyes, comfort, and gaze upon us. Read this fine collection—you will see for yourself.

—Gary Margolis, 2014 May Sarton New Hampshire Poetry Prize judge and author of *Raking the Winter Leaves.*

Desirée Alvarez won the 2015 May Sarton New Hampshire Poetry Prize. She is a poet and painter who has received numerous awards for her written and visual work, including the Glenna Luschei Award from *Prairie Schooner,* the Robert D. Richardson Non-Fiction Award from *Denver Quarterly,* and the Willard L. Metcalf Award from the American Academy of Arts and Letters. She has published in *Poetry, Boston Review,* and *The Iowa Review,* and received fellowships from Yaddo, Poets House, and New York Foundation for the Arts. Alvarez received her MFA from School of Visual Arts and BA from Wesleyan University. Testing the boundaries of image and language through interdisciplinary work, as a visual poet she exhibits widely and teaches at CUNY, The Juilliard School, and Artists Space.

These poems often shot shivers up my spine. Some made me cry.
This is a book I'll want to read over and over.

—Mekeel McBride, 2015 May Sarton New Hampshire Poetry Prize judge and author of *Dog Star Delicatessen: New and Selected Poems*

Zeina Hashem Beck won the 2016 May Sarton New Hampshire Poetry Prize. *Louder than Hearts* melds English and Arabic, focusing on language throughout.

Beck is a Lebanese poet. Her first collection, *To Live in Autumn*, won the 2013 Backwaters Prize; her chapbook, *3arabi Song* (2016), won the 2016 Rattle Chapbook Prize, and her chapbook, *There Was and How Much There Was* (2016), was a smith|doorstop Laureate's Choice, selected by Carol Ann Duffy. Her work has won Best of the Net, been nominated for the Pushcart Prize, the Forward Prize, and appeared in *Ploughshares, Poetry,* and *The Rialto,* among others. She lives in Dubai and performs her poetry both in the Middle East and internationally.

> "I don't know how Zeina Hashem Beck is able to do this. Her poems feel like whole worlds. Potent conversations with the self, the soul, the many landscapes of being, and the news that confounds us all—her poems weave two languages into a perfect fabric of presence, with an almost mystical sense of pacing and power."
>
> –Naomi Shihab Nye

Jen Town won the 2017 May Sarton New Hampshire Poetry Prize. *The Light of What Comes After* is an autobiographical mosaic of memory and dreams that speaks to all of us trying to make some semblance of aging and what it means to live well. Jen Town's poetry has appeared in *Mid-American Review, Cimarron Review, Epoch, Third Coast, Lake Effect, Crab Orchard Review, Unsplendid, Bellingham Review,* and others. Born in Dunkirk, New York and growing up in Erie, Pennsylvania, Town went on to earn her MFA in Creative Writing from The Ohio State University in 2008. She lives in Columbus, Ohio, with her wife, Carrie.

"*The Light of What Comes After* offers a sure manifesto against the domestic and cosmetic. Town's rich linguistic moments and surprising imagery lend her voice a slant which can seem playful and unafraid, but warning is always stitched just below the surface. This is a writer who knows 'Your debts / are more than you'll ever pay back.'"

—Jennifer Militello, 2017 May Sarton New Hampshire Poetry Prize judge and author of *A Camouflage of Specimens and Garments*

Marilee Richards won the 2018 May Sarton New Hampshire Poetry Prize. Richards learned poetry from Charles Entrekin and others after she wandered into a workshop put on by the Berkeley, CA, Poet's Co-op in the eighties while working as an adoption interviewer for Alameda County. Richards attended the workshops for several years prior to the organization dissolving and her move to Arizona in 2001. Her poems have been published in many journals, including *The Yale Review, The Southern Review, Rattle, Poetry Northwest, The Journal*, and *The Sun*. She is the author of *A Common Ancestor* (Hip Pocket Press, 2000), and in 2016 she won the William Matthews Poetry Prize.

This is a poet with range—sympathies, anger, tragedy, other people, love, humor.... Richards writes unsentimental poems that road-trip through our times and look around at who is with us when we stop to fill up our cars at gas stations, [who] has been with us in offices ... she reminds us of what the country has gained in consciousness and freedom, ... what sorrows and suicides we have left necessarily behind, as the bus pulls up at the curb in the don't-you-get-it-yet years we have been motoring through lately.

—David Blair, judge of the 2018 May Sarton New Hampshire Poetry Prize, and author of *Friends with Dogs* and *Arsonville*

Dorsey Craft is a PhD candidate in poetry at Florida State University. In addition to winning the May Sarton New Hampshire Poetry Prize, she has published her first chapbook, *The Pirate Anne Bonny Dances the Tarantella,* (Cutbank, 2020). Her work has appeared in *Colorado Review, Crab Orchard Review, Greensboro Review, Massachusetts Review, Ninth Letter, Passages North, Poetry Daily, Southern Indiana Review, Thrush Poetry Journal* and elsewhere. She holds an MFA in poetry from McNeese State University and is the Poetry Editor for *The Southeast Review.*

You will love Dorsey Craft's rollicking persona, pirate Anne Bonny, who serves up heaps of scintillant treasures from the bottomless trunk of her imagination, wit, and verve. In *Plunder,* Jack Sparrow has met his match.

—Deb Gorlin, judge, 2019 May Sarton New Hampshire Poetry Prize, and author of *Life of the Garment.*

In *Plunder* Dorsey Craft creates a ripple in the time-space continuum and brings 17th century pirate Anne Bonny to the 21st century. In these intense and erotic poems Bonny's wild and passionate life finds a place in the heart and mind of a contemporary woman and her struggle for love and freedom. This is a luminous and lyric debut.

—Barbara Hamby, author of *Bird Odyssey*

ALEXA DORAN is the 2020 winner of the May Sarton New Hampshire Poetry Prize and is the author of the chapbook, *Nightsink, Faucet Me a Lullaby* (Bottlecap Press 2019). She is currently a PhD candidate at Florida State University.

Her series of poems about the women of Dada, "The Octopus Breath on Her Neck," was recently released as part of Oxidant/Engine's BoxSet Series Vol 2.

You can also look for work from Doran in recent or issues of *Los Angeles Review*, *Mud Season Review*, *Salamander*, *Pithead Chapel* and *New Delta Review*, among others. She lives with her son in Tallahassee, Florida

Alexa Doran's *DM Me, Mother Darling* begins with a quote from J. M. Barrie's *Peter Pan*, in which little Michael asks his mother, "Can anything harm us?" Throughout the book, Mother Darling, who has lost her children, and the mother of a young boy, who tries to prepare her son for the world, speak to this seemingly ordinary question. However, as titles such as "Mother Darling Smokes a Spliff" and "For My Son, Who Asks Me to Replay Lizzo's 'Juice'" suggest, Doran casts these two women in wildly imaginative and compelling scenarios. The result is a book full of wit and wisdom. I can't recall the last time that a debut poetry collection made me laugh so hard or filled me with such surprise and wonder.

—Blas Falconer, author of *Forgive the Body This Failure*

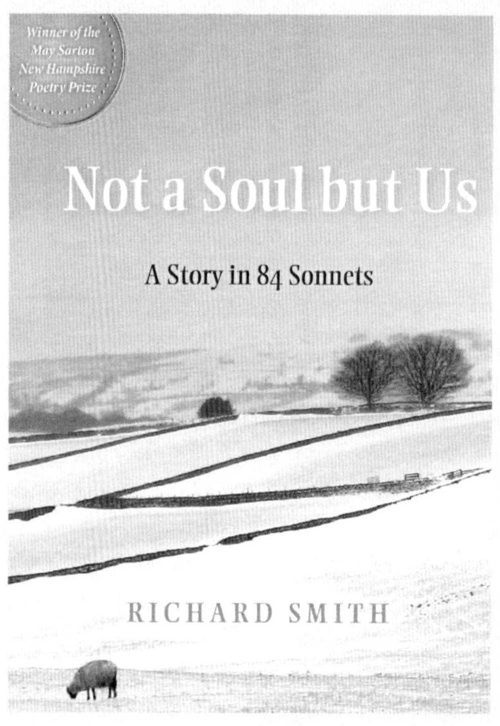

RICHARD SMITH is the 2021 winner of the May Sarton New Hampshire Poetry Prize and this is his first book of poetry. He began life as an English major. After graduating from Princeton, he worked in publishing for twelve years. In his thirties, he retooled as a clinical psychologist, earning his Ph.D. from the University of Maryland, College Park, and he now maintains a private practice in Washington, D.C.

He and his partner live with their two dogs, who inspired the sonnet-writing that led to this book.

Judge Meg Kearney says of Richard's work: "*Not a Soul But Us* is an achievement on every front. Set in rural England during and after the bubonic plague pandemic of 1348–49, this verse novel drives to the heart of what we humans are capable of when boiled down to our very core in the struggle to survive—and how, in more ways than one, it's not our intelligence or our resiliency but love and the non-human animals that save us. Timely, remarkable, and unforgettable, these eighty-four sonnets are so well crafted that we cease to notice the form, swept away as we are by the current of the story and its song."

Not since A. E. Housman's 1896 *The Shropshire Lad* has a poet produced such an endearing classic as *Not a Soul but Us* . . . Told in spare, authentic language reflecting the Anglo-Saxon world of Medieval Yorkshire, the sequence describes an orphaned boy and his dog who bond to survive, along with their sheep, during and after the bubonic plague. Each sonnet flows into the next with a natural cadence; readers will pause on the masterful couplets.

—Paula Deitz, editor of *The Hudson Review*

CATHERINE ARNOLD is the winner of the 2022 May Sarton New Hampshire Poetry Prize. Her debut collection, *Receipt for Lost Words,* plunges readers into a world of uncomfortable, deeply necessary truth-telling. With each poem, she invites us into a world of authenticity and awe, unearthing what's sacred in the casual miracles that other parents take for granted. Through compelling metaphor and painstaking detail, she conjures magical worlds in these pages. With beautiful simplicity and keen observation of what is seen and unseen, Arnold illustrates the fierce loyalty and elemental depth of a mother's love. These are poems that will stay with you because they take on poetry's most vital work: to say what will not—or cannot—be said. A stunning debut.

In *Receipt for Lost Words,* Catherine Arnold writes, "My daughter possessed it once / (speech) / and then she lost it / how will it be for us to dwell in a wordless land?" In this probing debut collection, the speaker interrogates the power and limits of language in a quest to understand her daughter's experience of the world. The result is a wonder of cerebral lyricism, an essayist's sustained attention paired with a poet's image-centered consciousness. Beyond "all the pinecone words / the kindling of manageable thoughts," this book blazes its hard, human fire. This is riveting work—hard, beautiful, necessary work.

—Julie Marie Wade, author of *Skirted* and *Just an Ordinary Woman Breathing*

Auguries
&
Divinations

Poems

HEATHER TRESELER

HEATHER TRESELER is the winner of the 2023 May Sarton New Hampshire Poetry Prize. In her collection *Auguries & Divinations,* Heather Treseler tracks a young woman's coming of age, attuned to the unspoken liabilities of women's lives, the suburban underworld, and the energies of eros. An older woman becomes the narrator's Beatrice in love and survival, and she returns to the New England of her childhood ready to claim a life of her own making, drawing on the classical practice of augury, or observing birds to discern human fate.

Poems in the collection have received prizes from *Narrative, Missouri Review, Frontier Poetry,* and the W. B. Yeats Society. Brad Crenshaw, in choosing the collection for the contest prize, noted: "Heather Treseler is compelling. We immediately want to listen to her the way we might listen to a lyric singer full of melody and rhythm. But make no mistake, running through all her lyricism is a staring, unblinking intelligence that informs us about what she sees. Her vision is inclusive, generous, wide-ranging, and enthralling."

It has been years since I have read a new poet of such rhetorical sophistication and mastery. Wow. One thinks of the young Robert Lowell. Rhetorical mastery fueled by fury and necessity. Agony shaped and released by intelligence, by art. A breathtaking debut.

—Frank Bidart